THE USE C NIDDERDALE MAF OTHER CRINOIDAL LIMESTONES IN FOUNTAINS ABBEY, NORTH YORKSHIRE

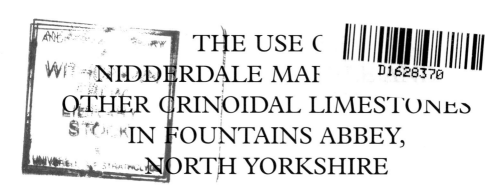

by

J. G. Blacker

High Harefield Cottage, Ripon Road, Pateley Bridge,
Harrogate HG3 5DG, Yorkshire

and

M. Mitchell

Department of Earth Sciences, University of Leeds LS2 9JT, Yorkshire

THE LEEDS PHILOSOPHICAL AND LITERARY SOCIETY LTD

JUNE 1998

Proceedings of the Leeds Philosophical and Literary Society, Scientific Section, Vol. XII, Part 1, pp. 1-28

The Leeds Philosophical and Literary Society Ltd
City Museum
Calverley Street
Leeds LS1 3AA

Editor, Scientific Section
DR H. M. PANTIN
University of Leeds

British Library Cataloguing-in-Publication Data:
a catalogue record for this book is available from the British Library.

ISBN: 1-870737-14-8

Printed in Great Britain by
Fretwell Print and Design, Goulbourne Street, Keighley, West Yorkshire BD21 1PZ

THE USE OF NIDDERDALE MARBLE AND OTHER CRINOIDAL LIMESTONES IN FOUNTAINS ABBEY, NORTH YORKSHIRE

by J. G. Blacker and M. Mitchell

SUMMARY

Crinoidal limestones of Lower Carboniferous (Dinantian) age were widely used during medieval times as decorative stones in the churches and abbeys of Northern England. A variety of this distinctive stone, known as Nidderdale Marble, was used in Fountains Abbey, situated four miles south-west of Ripon, North Yorkshire. Two types have been recognised. Little is now left in situ, and this paper, combining reference information from English Heritage with an examination of material, in situ or in store, describes the locations within the Abbey complex where the marble was used, and relates this to the chronology of construction. No documentation identifying the locality of the source quarry has yet been found but, using historical and geological evidence, a quarry at Lofthouse, in Nidderdale, is suggested as the most likely site.

Fountains Abbey, and neighbouring Fountains Hall, where material was recycled from the Abbey, are at present the only known buildings where the stone was used.

Two other varieties of crinoidal limestone, very different in character to Nidderdale Marble, not previously documented in the Abbey, have been observed. Their source is unknown.

The authors would welcome any further information on the source and other uses of Nidderdale Marble, and the other crinoidal limestones discussed.

INTRODUCTION

Enhancement of the visual appearance of the internal fabric of medieval churches, abbeys and monasteries was common practice, using painted decoration or stone contrasting with the colour and texture of the basic structure.

Purbeck Marble from Dorset, perhaps the most familiar of the decorative stone types, was widely used not only in the south of England but also in many northern churches, Beverley Minster being a notable example. Frosterley Marble, from Weardale in County Durham, is another example, seen at its best in the magnificent setting of the Chapel of The Nine Altars in Durham Cathedral.

Less well appreciated is Nidderdale Marble and its extensive use in Fountains Abbey, North Yorkshire (Figure 1). Founded in 1132, by the Cistercian Order, Fountains rapidly became the principal house of the Order in England, acquiring large estates not only in Yorkshire, but extending to the Lake District. Wealth was accumulated by astute management, particularly of agricultural interests, along with grants and endowments made by those wishing to ensure spiritual longevity.

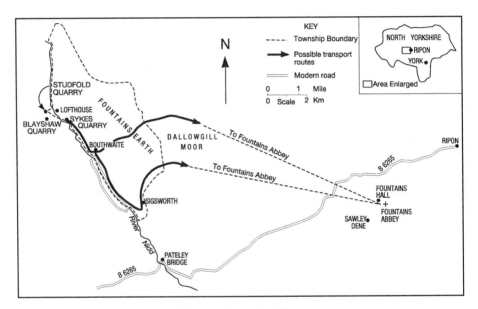

Figure 1. Location Map.

The structures of the Fountains complex were mainly built of sandstone blocks, from the Lower Plompton Grit (Millstone Grit) of Namurian age, quarried from cliffs on the side of the valley of the River Skell, immediately to the north of the Abbey. By 1250 all the major buildings were complete, although many modifications and renovations were carried out over the following centuries. Following the dissolution of Fountains Abbey in 1539, the removal of lead roofing, and deliberate despoliation of the Abbey buildings, decay set in and the fine decoration within the Abbey, including features made of Nidderdale Marble, lost their earlier grandeur. John Leland in his grand tour visited Fountains Abbey in the early 1540s and commented on the many black marble columns, with black and white specks interspersed, to be found in the Chapter House, Refectory and New Altar in the eastern part of the Church (Walbran 1862).

Today very little marble is left in situ, but many items are preserved both in the Abbey Museum, and in the archive stone stores administered by English Heritage.

A glossary of architectural terms is appended.

CRINOIDS AND CRINOIDAL LIMESTONES

Crinoidal limestones are notoriously variable, due to the form of crinoids and the way that beds of this kind of limestone were deposited. Sometimes known as sea lilies, crinoids belong to the animal Phylum Echinoderma, and are related to sea urchins and starfish. They are common as rock-forming fossils in the Palaeozoic age, less common in the Mesozoic, and rare in the Cenozoic. However, crinoids are still living today, with their maximum occurrence in warm-sea environments such as the Great Barrier Reef of Australia.

Crinoids consist of a more or less flexible stem, up to a metre or more in length, usually rooted into the sea bed, with a cup or calyx at the top, and movable arms growing from the margin of the cup. They feed by filtering minute organisms from sea water. A living crinoid consists of a calcareous skeleton, bound together and surrounded by organic tissue. The stem of the skeleton consists of a number of disc-like segments or columnals, which have a central opening. The cup and arms are also formed by a series of plates. After death, the calcareous skeleton usually breaks into fragments. These pieces can often be identified by the shining cleavage faces of calcite crystals from which they are composed.

Many Lower Carboniferous limestones contain scattered broken fragments of crinoids, stem columnals being the commonest debris. However, under specially favourable conditions, for example near the edge of relatively shallow-water areas where nutrient-rich cold-water currents from deeper water occur, dense thickets of crinoids often grew. Under these conditions, the fragile crinoid skeletons were broken up and short lengths of stems and disarticulated fragments were sufficiently abundant to form richly-crinoidal deposits. These beds either accumulated where the crinoids grew, or more commonly the fragments were carried away by strong currents, and laid down in banks elsewhere. The strength of the currents was a major factor in determining the extent to which the stems broke up, the size of crinoid debris laid down, and the composition, nature and amount of matrix or cement in which the crinoid debris was deposited.

Being current-reworked bank deposits, richly-crinoidal limestones are very variable in composition, vertical thickness and lateral extent. It is this variable character which makes it difficult to identify the source of a specific crinoidal limestone with certainty. Many rocks rich in crinoids are dense enough to take a polish which accentuates the fossil content, and is retained when used in interior positions in buildings protected from weathering action. They are often referred to as "marbles". However, they are not in the geological sense true marbles, which are limestones metamorphosed by heat and pressure.

CRINOIDAL LIMESTONES IN FOUNTAINS ABBEY

Three distinct types of crinoidal material can be seen, in situ, within the Abbey (Figure 2). These will be referred to as Nidderdale Marble, signifying its origin from Nidderdale; Bird's Eye Marble; and Dark Eye Marble. The last two, whose origins are at present unknown, are new observations relating to the buildings of Fountains Abbey. Nidderdale Marble occurs in two lithologies, both of which have been found within the quarry suggested as the source of the stone.

KEY TO PLAN OF FOUNTAINS ABBEY
A. Nave
B. Central Tower
C. Choir
D. Presbytery
E. Chapel of The Nine Altars
F. Cloister
G. Sacristy
H. Chapter House
J. Refectory
K. Lay-Brothers' Refectory
L. Monk's Infirmary

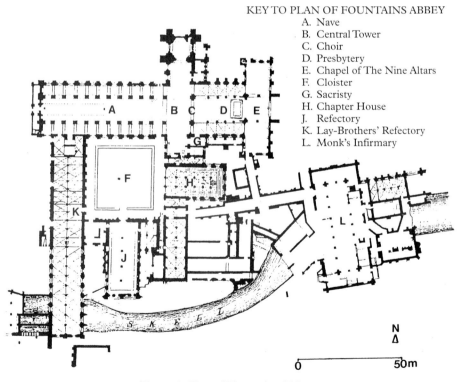

N
0   50m

Figure 2. Plan of Fountains Abbey.

Nidderdale Marble

This richly-crinoidal limestone was used in many phases of the building programme as an interior decorative stone and, in places, a structural stone. Two types (A and B) have been identified. The colour of quarried stone is mid-grey, but takes on a mid- to dark-grey colour when polished (rear cover).

Type A

This was the most extensively used variety.

The distinctive character of the stone is that the crinoid columnals are in two size ranges, 2-5 mm and 8-11 mm in diameter. The larger columnals tend to occur in stem sections 20 to 40 mm in length, with up to 70 mm recorded. The sediment in the centres of the columnals is the same colour as the rock matrix, and the rock is silicified. Small patches of quartz can be identified on the weathered surfaces of examples of Nidderdale Marble still in situ in the Abbey.

Nidderdale Marble cannot be positively identified in structures associated with the first phase of Abbey building of 1138-1150. However, examination of blocks in situ and in the English Heritage stone stores, combined with information from the English Heritage archive database, confirms the following later uses of this distinctive stone.

The first firm evidence of the use of the stone is in the Choir, built 1150-1170, where it was extensively used for abacuses, annulet rings, corbels and keeled shafts. None are now in situ but two superb examples of corbel brackets (Figure 3) are displayed in the Abbey Museum.

There is a grave slab, date unknown, in the Sacristy made from a single piece of this marble.

After the Church itself, the most important structure was the Chapter House. Reconstructed after a destructive fire of 1146, and in use by 1170, ten marble plinths, still in position, supported Nidderdale Marble columns, three of which survive. The columns had matching capitals; one of them is in the Abbey Museum. The columns, supporting the ceiling vaulting, were both decorative and structural.

The Central Tower, contemporary with Robert of Pipewell's abbacy, 1170-1180, contained shafts, capitals and abacuses of this marble.

Building of the Cloister Arcade has also been accredited to Abbot Robert and bases, capitals and shafts supporting arches of the arcade were all of Nidderdale Marble (English Heritage 1988; Gilyard-Beer 1978).

The Refectory, constructed 1170-1180, has several examples of Nidderdale Marble in situ. The doorway on the south side of the Cloister, leading into the Refectory, has remnants of column-base plinths. Within the Refectory, fragments of one of four columns that supported the ceiling, and its base, both in Nidderdale Marble, remain. The pulpit, on the west side, has base mouldings to nook shafts and, at the north end, a spacer between columns.

The north and south side arcades of the Presbytery, 1210-1220, were lined with free standing marble shafts, one of which, on the west end of the north side, still survives, and remnants of the polished surface can still be detected on the rear of the column (Figures 4,5). Still visible are many moulded annulets and abacuses above the main arcade. Their associated shafts are missing.

The main use of Nidderdale Marble, however, was in the Chapel of The Nine Altars, 1220-1250, the interior of which was richly decorated. Long shafts in clusters surrounding the main structural columns, and shafts flanking the windows, their bases, corbels and abacuses throughout this large building would have presented a magnificent sight (Figure 6). Today, all that remain in situ are corbels showing the distinctive features of crinoids on weathered surfaces, moulding rings, the southern border of the east window and one nook shaft high on the south side of this window.

Four capitals and free-standing shafts from the Screen Arcade which surrounded the High Altar in the Presbytery, not now in situ, date from the 1220-1250 period.

The 36 shafts that formed the spokes of the rose window at the east end, removed in 1483, were all marble (Coppack 1993).

Massive vault bosses for the ceiling between the Chapel of The Nine Altars and the Presbytery, of the 1220-1250 period, now in store, are another structural use of the stone.

Some of the finely-carved Nidderdale Marble pieces now in the Fountains Abbey stone store are worked in Type A limestone, with stem sections of the larger diameter (10+ mm) crinoid columnals.

Type B
The second of the two types of Nidderdale Marble was used for the quatrefoil-shaped bowl of the Holy Water Stoup, dating from 1220-1250, which was mounted on a sandstone base to the east of the processional door leading from the south aisle of the Abbey Nave into the Cloister. The intricately carved foliage surrounding the bowl is still sharp, and makes this one of the most beautiful of the Fountains Abbey treasures (Figure 7). The base remains in situ but the bowl is now in the English Heritage stone store at Helmsley (English Heritage 1988).

Carved from a block of crinoidal limestone, 32 cm deep and 52 cm maximum dimension, it differs from the Nidderdale Marble noted elsewhere (Type A), in that it consists of a fine-grained limestone with much broken coral, bryozoa, shell and crinoid debris. Small crinoid columnals ranging from 0.7-3 mm, but predominantly less than 2 mm, can be identified, but they are much damaged and corroded. Silicification is not apparent. The bowl lithology can be matched with that seen in the top part of one of the sliced and polished samples taken from the base of the Upper Leaf of the Five Yard Limestone exposed in the quarry suggested as the source of Nidderdale Marble (see below).

It is suggested here that Nidderdale Marble with long sections of crinoid columnals up to 70 cm and diameter 8-11 mm would not have been suitable for detailed carving. The random occurrence of these large crinoidal stems, which consist of easily fractured calcite crystals, could cause the stone to flake or break, foiling attempts to carve fine detail. Additionally, the visual impact of this bowl would have been impaired if large diameter crinoid columnals had been apparent on the surface to detract from the detail of the carving. A more even-textured material may therefore have been specially selected for the bowl. Its availability within the same quarry as Type A Nidderdale Marble would perhaps have encouraged the carving of this fine piece, and this indicates the great skill and experience of the stone masons of the time.

In addition to the Holy Water Stoup, seven finely-carved blocks of Type B Nidderdale Marble have been identified in the Fountains Abbey stone store. These are mostly shaft bases, and have sharp-edged flutings.

All items of Nidderdale Marble from the various phases of Abbey construction that have been examined, in situ and in the English Heritage stores, have lithologies that can be matched with either Type A or Type B limestone, both of which occur in the proposed source quarry (see below). This strongly suggests that one quarry only was used during the hundred years, 1150-1250, of major building activity. The considerable quantities of Type A material used, particularly in the Presbytery and Chapel of The Nine Altars, means that this quarry would have been extensive by medieval standards. To support the quarrying activities over this length of time a substantial working complex must have been created.

Bird's Eye Marble

A small amount of a very different crinoidal limestone has been used for the abacus blocks of both the north and south doorways of the Chapel of The Nine Altars (Figure 8).

An abacus is an important structural element which spreads the load of the masonry above. It is the top member of a capital upon which rests the weight of the wall above. In the present case, blocks on either side of the doorway are sandwiched between sandstones of the door arch and doorway. The source of this particular limestone is not known.

These abacuses are composed of fine-grained, argillaceous, dark-grey limestone which has weathered badly. They also contain rare scattered small (0.5-1 mm diameter) crinoid columnals; rare small angular fragments of black chert (5 x 6 mm to 5 x 13 mm in size); and one fragment of mid-grey coloured limestone (20 x 23 mm). The blocks are a uniform 80 mm thick and formed of large slabs with dimensions of 1-1.15 x 0.7-0.9 metres. Although it is possible that they were worked by splitting blocks, it is more probable that they are from an 80 mm thick bed. No beds of limestone with the character of these abacus blocks have been seen in the Lower Carboniferous outcrops in Nidderdale. The presence of small crinoid columnals in a dark limestone suggests that this may be an example of a variety of decorative stone found in other localities, and known as Bird's Eye Marble.

Dark-grey or black limestones of Lower Carboniferous age are widely used as decorative stones, and most of them are from Ireland, Tournai in Belgium, or Ashford-in-the-Water, near Bakewell, Derbyshire. Much of the Ashford stone is pure black when polished, with no included fragments. However, the limestones from small mines in Nettler Dale, about 1 mile west of Ashford, contain scattered small crinoid columnals and are known as Derbyshire Bird's Eye Marble (Tomlinson 1996). A similar black limestone with small crinoid columnals was worked in Dent Dale, Cumbria, and is known as Dent Black Marble.

It should be stressed that without documentary evidence regarding the stones used for the abacus slabs of the Chapel of The Nine Altars at Fountains Abbey, it is impossible to identify their origin. All that can be said is that they are a variety of Bird's Eye limestone, possibly from the Lower Carboniferous of the Pennines.

Two additional pieces of Bird's Eye-like limestone have been identified amongst the material in the Fountains Abbey stone store. The English Heritage database records these as abacus slabs from the Choir Clerestory Arcade, dating from 1150-1170. These slabs have dimensions of 53.5 x 42.5 cm and 65 x 30.5 cm and are both 9 cm thick. Composed of dark-grey argillaceous limestone, the block bases are unweathered, but the upper surfaces are flaking. Small crinoid columnals, mainly less than 2 mm but up to 5 mm in diameter, are present. One slab contains a fragment of mid-grey limestone, and the other has two coral fragments, one of which is a *Dibunophyllum bipartitum* (McCoy). No chert nodules were seen. This lithology is very similar to that of the Chapel of The Nine Altars doorway abacuses, and may be the same stone.

Finding additional pieces of this limestone makes it more likely that the material referred to as Bird's Eye Marble was worked from the same quarry as the two types of Nidderdale Marble (A and B), but from beds which are not now exposed.

Dark Eye Marble

Another variety of crinoidal limestone, the source of which is not known but is probably not Nidderdale, has dark centres to the columnal stems. This can be found, in situ, in abacuses supporting the arch of the doorway leading from the Cloister into the Lay-Brothers' Refectory (Figures 9,10).

The doorway passes through a wall comprising two phases of construction. The side within this Refectory is of roughly-worked sandstone blocks and dates from about 1138-1150, the period of construction of the first stone buildings of the Abbey. The Cloister side is built of better-worked blocks and dates from when the Cloister was reconstructed, between about 1150 and 1170 (Coppack & Gilyard-Beer 1995). There is conflicting evidence of the date of the doorway itself. The ground plans accompanying St. John Hope's (1900) and Gilyard-Beer's (1978) histories of the Abbey appear to indicate a date around 1150. It has, however, been recently suggested that the doorway dates from about 1170-1180 (Coppack & Gilyard-Beer 1995).

Another use of this variety of Marble was in the Monk's Infirmary, originally built during the same phase as the Chapel of The Nine Altars, 1220-1250. Cluster shafts supported by moulded collars surround the piers that supported the Hall ceiling (Figures 11,12). These may not, however, be original, and possibly were made at the time of reconstruction of this building in the 19th century. The shafts are made up of between three and five sections.

NIDDERDALE MARBLE QUARRIES

Limestones of Lower Carboniferous age crop out in small areas in the Upper Nidd Valley (Wilson 1960), and all likely Nidderdale Marble quarry sites have been visited during the present investigation. Sykes Quarry (see below) is considered to be the source of the large quantities of crinoidal limestone, generally referred to as Nidderdale Marble, used in Fountains Abbey, and possibly also Bird's Eye Marble.

Sykes Quarry (SE107729)

This quarry, cartographically unnamed but here referred to as Sykes Quarry, from the name of the adjacent former grange of Fountains Abbey, is located on the north side of the River Nidd, near Lofthouse. It is close

Figure 3. A corbel bracket. Displayed in Abbey Museum.

Figure 4. Shaft in situ in north arcade of Presbytery.

Figure 5. Presbytery shaft, close up to show crinoid fragments.

Figure 6. Chapel of The Nine Altars from the south.

Figure 7. Holy Water Stoup. English Heritage stone store at Helmsley. Accession No. 78206212.

Figure 8. South doorway to the Chapel of The Nine Altars showing the abacus blocks of Bird's Eye Marble.

Figure 9. Doorway from Cloister into Lay-Brothers' Refectory.

Figure 10. Close up of abacus of Doorway from Cloister into Lay-Brothers' Refectory.

Figure 11. Cluster shafts and pier in Monk's Infirmary.

Figure 12. Close up of cluster shaft on pier in Monk's Infirmary.

to the southernmost limit of the Lower Carboniferous outcrops in
Nidderdale. Several very large trees now grow in the quarry and it is
estimated that it, and a small adjacent limekiln, have been defunct for at
least 200 years.

The exposed face is about 50 metres long and 3 metres high, with an
unknown thickness covered by debris. A sandstone quarry in the
Grassington Grit (Namurian) succession lies immediately above the
quarry, and it is likely that debris from this site has obscured as much as
100 metres of additional old workings to the east of the exposed quarry
section (Mr I.C.Burgess, personal communication 1996).

The limestone in Sykes Quarry is in two main Leaves or parts, separated
by beds of cherty mudstone and chert. This arrangement of beds is typical
of the Five Yard Limestone found near Lofthouse, in the Nidd valley to
the north of the quarry, and in How Stean Gorge to the northwest.

The geological section through Sykes Quarry is as follows (Dr A.
A.Wilson, personal communication 1997).

	Metres
Mudstone	seen to 0.80
FIVE YARD LIMESTONE	
UPPER LEAF	
Medium grey crinoidal limestone (grainstone, grain supported, with little or no fine-grained matrix); thickens to south.	0.48 to 0.74
Medium grey, richly-crinoidal limestone (Type A; grainstone, overlain sharply by Type B; packstone-wackestone, partly grain supported, partly grains floating in a fine-grained matrix between the grains, thins to south); this bed has been sampled and polished (see below).	0.11 to 0.28
Uneven surface.	
Cherty, platy limestone, passing laterally into limestone.	0.07
Chert and cherty limestone, irregularly weathering in top half.	0.45
Cherty mudstone.	0.20
LOWER LEAF	
Medium dark-grey, slightly siliceous limestone.	0.35 to 0.45
Clayey mudstone.	0.01
Medium to pale-grey limestone in four beds (packstone to crinoidal grainstone), no base seen.	1.05 to 1.15

The Upper Leaf of the Five Yard Limestone in Sykes Quarry is rich in crinoid columnals. A cut and polished sample from the basal bed (rear cover), shows it to be a medium-grey coloured limestone. In the lower part of this bed (Type A) the crinoid grains largely rest on each other with minimal fine-grained matrix, making a grainstone. The columnals have sharp edges and are of two sizes. The smaller ones are common throughout and range from 2 to 5 mm in diameter; the larger ones are less common, ranging from 8 to 11 mm in diameter and are variable in distribution. Articulated sections of stem columnals are also present towards the base and are between 20 and 50 mm in length. This is the lithology most commonly found in Fountains Abbey and is noted as Nidderdale Marble Type A.

A conspicuous feature of the lower part of the basal bed (Type A) is the presence of small patches of blue-grey silica, which also infills the centres of some of the crinoid columnals. This is probably secondary-replacement mineralisation associated with the major east-west Lofthouse Fault, which occurs about 100 metres to the south of the quarry. Silicification makes this a very hard limestone which is difficult to break even with a heavy hammer. Silica in the form of chert nodules is present in several limestones in the Lower Carboniferous of the Pennines, but the silicification present in this quarry has not been seen in any other crinoidal limestone locally. It may be that this character is unique, providing a very useful diagnostic feature to allow correlation of material in Fountains Abbey with Sykes Quarry.

This lower unit is overlain, with a sharp contact, by a packstone-wackestone (Type B) composed of fewer and smaller crinoid columnal fragments (0.7-3 mm but mostly less than 2 mm in diameter) which are broken and corroded, some grains supporting, some floating in a matrix of mud and comminuted siltgrade debris (shell, crinoid, coral and bryozoa). There are no large (8-11 mm) crinoid columnals in this lithology, and an etched surface shows the matrix to be silicified. This upper portion of the basal bed is found in the Holy Water Stoup and for some other finely-carved pieces. It is referred to as Nidderdale Marble Type B.

Stone that is quarried for building or decorative use, unless it is a very massive freestone that can be worked in any direction, requires to have natural fractures which facilitate, and may also determine, the manner of working. Given that a sequence of rocks has bedding of a sufficient thickness for its intended use, the spacing of the joints is a vitally important feature, and controls the size of the blocks that can be quarried. Two sets of joints are present in the limestone of Sykes Quarry; the direction of one is almost north-south (004° from grid north) and that of the other is east-west (274°). In the Upper Leaf beds, the north-south set has a spacing between 0.44 and 1.50 metres, and the east-west set between 0.57 and 1.70 metres. The largest block in the present exposed quarry face measures 1.50 by 1.70 metres. In the thinner bedded Lower Leaf, the joints are more widely spaced, and would allow blocks measuring up to 1.80 by 5.60 metres to be extracted.

Within the likely variation of Lower Carboniferous crinoidal-bank deposits, the crinoidal limestones of Fountains Abbey, referred to as Type A and Type B Nidderdale Marble, have much in common with the lithologies examined from Sykes Quarry.

The historical background to development of land ownership by the Abbey lends support to the opinion that this is the most likely source of the material. At the time of the earliest suggested use of Nidderdale Marble in the Choir of the Abbey, 1150-1170, rights for minerals, lead, iron and stone, had been granted to Fountains within the Forest of Nidderdale, an area which included the site of Sykes Quarry. No bounds were defined at this time but, in 1176, a more specific grant was made giving very precisely the boundaries of the land awarded to the Abbey (Greenway 1972). The Abbot of Byland however, also claimed rights over much of the same land immediately to the north of the quarry, and agreement was only reached, in favour of Fountains, in 1198 (Lancaster 1915, Volume 1; Jennings 1983). As the quarry was outside the disputed area Fountains stone working activities could proceed unimpeded. The township on which Sykes Quarry is situated became known as Fountains Earth.

Thus, by the time the stone was in major demand for the decoration and construction of Presbytery and Chapel of The Nine Altars, 1210-1250, the quarry site was securely within the ownership of the Abbot of Fountains, although the geological evidence indicates that the same quarry also supplied stone for the earlier building phases.

Routeways out of Nidderdale (Figure 1), only traversing land held by Fountains, via Bouthwaite or Sigsworth and across Dallowgill Moor, could be used to transport stone the eleven miles (18 kilometres) from quarry to Abbey (Lancaster 1915, Volume 1). Agreements, and disputes, with other land owners were therefore avoided.

The geological and historical evidence strongly supports the proposal that both types of Nidderdale Marble for Fountains Abbey came from Sykes Quarry.

Blayshaw Quarry (SE098729)

A relatively small quarry, close to Blayshaw Gill, on the south side of the River Nidd, also near Lofthouse, is reputed locally to have been the source of Nidderdale Marble used in Fountains Abbey. It was worked spasmodically from the late 19th century to the 1930s, and the stone, for example, was used for the war memorials at Summerbridge and Ramsgill (Blacker 1996).

This quarry worked the Middle Limestone which underlies the Five Yard Limestone. The Middle Limestone here is pale-grey coloured, and made up almost entirely of broken fragments of crinoid columnals, 2 to 6.5 mm in diameter, the margins of which have been abraded. Comparison of this stone with the three crinoidal limestones used in the Abbey indicates that Blayshaw Quarry is not the source of any of them.

Historically, land in the Forest of Nidderdale on which the quarry is situated was part of an easement which included rights to minerals, made to Byland Abbey between about 1147-1154. Fountains, as mentioned earlier, also had access to minerals within the same area. However, stone was not included in the Byland grant, as it was to Fountains in about 1151. Precise land bounds of the Byland awards were not defined until about 1160-1172, thus perhaps ending difficulties which must have arisen for the Abbot of Fountains in interpreting the freedoms granted within the estate of the Forest of Nidderdale (Greenway 1972).

During the major period of use of Nidderdale Marble in Fountains Abbey, Blayshaw Quarry site was indisputably within Byland Abbey's Nidderdale estates. It seems very unlikely that Fountains would wish to negotiate an agreement to extract and to transport across Byland lands when they had ready access to the prized stone in their own quarry. In addition, no evidence has been found in Byland Abbey of crinoidal limestones from Nidderdale or any other locality.

The combination of geological and historic evidence suggests that Blayshaw Quarry was not exploited at any time by Fountains Abbey for Nidderdale Marble.

Other exposures of crinoidal limestones, which have been quarried for lime burning, occur in the vicinity of Lofthouse. Close to Thwaite House (SE101765) there is a small quarry, but the rock face is highly jointed, making it totally unsuitable for uses requiring uniform, fracture free, lengths of bed. Valuation lists of property and land in Stonebeck Down township (Nidderdale Museum Archives; 1871, 1875) show that Studfold Quarry (SE097733) was also involved with lime burning.

From whatever source, the stone would, almost certainly, have been roughly worked on site prior to transporting to a mason's workshop close to Fountains Abbey. Sawley Dene was an area with several quarries owned by the Abbot, including one which supplied millstones, and it is possible that the marble was polished at this stone-working site. Thomas, the marble mason of Sawley, is mentioned in grants made to the monks in the first half of the thirteenth century (Walbran 1862; Lancaster 1915, Volume 2).

DISCUSSION AND CONCLUSIONS

A re-examination of geological and historical evidence suggests that the two types of stone called Nidderdale Marble (Types A and B), which have been identified in Fountains Abbey, came from a quarry, near Lofthouse, here called Sykes Quarry, within the land holding of Fountains Abbey. It is likely to have been the sole source of this marble, and to have been at its most active between 1170 and 1250, although the evidence suggests the same source for the earlier phases of construction. It is suggested that the name SYKES MARBLE be used for these limestones to recognise their provenance, and to avoid confusion with other examples of crinoidal limestone from Nidderdale.

Blayshaw Quarry, situated on land within Byland Abbey's guardianship, is very unlikely to have been the source, as has often been previously supposed. Details of the Blayshaw crinoidal limestone are not consistent with material either in situ in the Abbey, or in the English Heritage stone stores.

The Sykes Marble occurs in two types. That which was most extensively used (Type A) is richly crinoidal and has columnals in two size ranges. It is a very hard stone and this is partly due to the presence of secondarily deposited patches of blue-grey coloured silica, a feature which may be diagnostic of this particular stone.

The second (Type B), noted in the Holy Water Stoup, and some other delicately carved stones, is a fine-grained material with only small crinoid columnals, and shell, crinoid, coral and bryozoa debris.

A forthcoming paper will discuss the physical and mechanical characteristics of some polishable stones and will include reference to Sykes Marble (Moyes and others, in preparation).

A different limestone was used for the abacus slabs of the north and south doorways of the Chapel of The Nine Altars, and for some Choir abacuses. This is a fine-grained, dark-grey coloured material with scattered small crinoid columnals, which has weathered badly, and is a limestone variety known as Bird's Eye Marble. Although the source of this stone has not been identified, it is possible that it came from beds in Sykes Quarry that are no longer exposed.

A third variety of crinoidal limestone, here called Dark Eye Marble, because of the dark centres to the crinoid columnals, has been identified in the Infirmary and in abacuses of the doorway leading from the Cloister into the Lay-Brothers' Refectory. The source has not been established, but is probably not Nidderdale.

ACKNOWLEDGEMENTS

Andrew Morrison of English Heritage has allowed access to the stone stores within his care. Our very grateful thanks to him, Kate Wilson and Keith Emerick, also of English Heritage, for their interest and support. Tony Moyes and John Walker have made valuable comments on the history and architecture of the Abbey. Iain Burgess and Albert Wilson, both formerly with the British Geological Survey, have helped interpret details of the geology and have given freely of their knowledge and time. Steve Moorhouse's knowledge of the medieval landscape has been invaluable.

The black and white photographs were printed by University of Leeds Photographic Section; the support of the Department of Earth Sciences for this work is acknowledged. The photograph of the Holy Water Stoup (Figure 7), taken by Bob Smith, is reproduced with the permission of English Heritage. All other photographs are from the authors' collection. The drawing of Figure 1 by Jerry Hodgson is acknowledged.

Many others have been involved and our thanks to all.

REFERENCES

BLACKER, J. G. (1996) The Stone Industry of Nidderdale - Part 2: Stone uses. *British Mining* No.57: 5-33.

COPPACK, G. (1993) *Fountains Abbey*. Batsford Limited & English Heritage, London.

COPPACK, G. & GILYARD-BEER, R. (1995) *Fountains Abbey*. English Heritage, London.

ENGLISH HERITAGE. (1988) *Abbeys: Yorkshire's Monastic Heritage*. Published by English Heritage for the exhibition held at the Yorkshire Museum, York from 31 March to 31 October 1988.

GILYARD-BEER, R. (1978) *Fountains Abbey, North Yorkshire*. H.M.S.O., London.

GREENWAY, D. E., ed. (1972) *Charters of the Honour of Mowbray*. Oxford University Press, 40-98.

JENNINGS, B., ed. (1983) *A history of Nidderdale*. 2nd Edition. Nidderdale History Group: 43.

LANCASTER, W. T., ed. (1915) *Abstracts of the Charters and other documents contained in the Chartulary of the Cistercian Abbey of Fountains*. Leeds: privately printed. Volume 1: 215-216 & Volume 2: 618-624.

MOYES, A. J., KNOTT, P. & NAVARETTA, L. (in preparation) Stones as polishable materials.

ST. JOHN HOPE, W. H. (1900) Fountains Abbey, Yorkshire. *Yorkshire Archaeological Journal* **15**: 1-134.

TOMLINSON, J. M. (1996) *Derbyshire Black Marble, with appendices* by *Trevor D. Ford*. Peak District Mines Historical Society, Special Publication No.4.

WALBRAN, J. R. (1862) Memorials of the Abbey of St. Mary of Fountains. *Surtees Society* **42**: 129.

WILSON, A. A. (1960) The Carboniferous rocks of Coverdale and adjacent valleys in the Yorkshire Pennines. *Proceedings of the Yorkshire Geological Society* **32**: 285-316.

GLOSSARY OF ARCHITECTURAL TERMS

ABACUS Upper member of a capital, supporting a wall or arch above

AISLE Part of a church on either side of the nave or chancel. An aisle is usually separated from the nave by an arcade

ANNULET A ring round a circular pier or shaft

CAPITAL The uppermost part of a column or shaft, usually carved or decorated

CHANCEL Eastern part of a church reserved for clergy and choir

CHAPTER HOUSE The room where the monks met for every day monastic business and to listen to a reading from the monastic rule

CHOIR Part of a church between the nave and the presbytery, occupied by the choristers

CLERESTORY Upper structure rising above the level of the roof of the aisle and containing windows to let light into the centre of the church

CLOISTER Covered walkway round an open quadrangle (or garth), which links the central monastic buildings with the church

COLUMN A cylindrical, square or polygonal vertical pillar, usually supporting an arch

CORBEL A stone bracket projecting from a wall to support another feature, such as an arch

INFIRMARY A room or hall to accommodate sick members of a monastery, or their guests if taken ill

NAVE Western arm or main body of a church extending westwards from the crossing

PRESBYTERY Part of the eastern arm of a church between the choir and the high altar, usually reserved for the clergy, and including the high altar

REFECTORY Monastic, communal dining room

SACRISTY Place for keeping the sacred vessels and vestments

SHAFT Column between base and capital: usually cylindrical, but sometimes KEELED with curved faces meeting at a ridge; if in a recess referred to as a NOOK shaft

STOUP A basin containing holy water

TRANSEPT The north and south transverse arms of a cruciform church

VAULT An arched stone or brick roof of a ceiling, often supported with decorative ribs